Musings of a Wandering Mind

Gabrielle Skrzypek

BookLeaf Publishing

India | USA | UK

Presentation by *BookLeaf Publishing*

Web: www.bookleafpub.com

E-mail: info@bookleafpub.com

ISBN: 9789363302389

First edition 2024

ACKNOWLEDGEMENT

This work would not have been possible without some very key players!

To BookLeaf Publishing: thank you for your hard work in giving writers like me the chance to push themselves, work hard, and achieve publication!

To every English teacher whose class I had growing up: thank you for giving me a deep love of literature and the beauty of the written word, especially poetry. You put each beloved book in my hands and taught me to see them as my own personal adventure.

To every Art teacher: thank you for showing students like me the beauty of life that art can capture in various mediums. Whether written, painted, sung, or acted, art tells the story of all of us!

To my friends: thanks for still being willing to be seen in public with me despite every odd quirk!

To my family: thank you for every day of love, support, patience, and inspiration! I couldn't do anything without you, and I hope I always make you proud!

To the Lord God who gives every good gift and talent! May these words and musings give Him continuous praise!

PREFACE

"Yet God has made everything beautiful for its own time."
~Ecclesiastes 3:11 (NLT)

"God is the perfect poet."
~Robert Browning

The Meaning of Family

Fresh soil,
Tilled,
Tended,
Cared for to see the best of ourselves grow,
A garden sown in understanding, compassion,
and gentleness.

Artwork,
Painted,
Protected,
Preserved in defense of beauty in us,
A canvas filled with the vibrancy of kindness,
grace, and joy.

Musical Notes,
Composed,
Conducted,
Shared to bring belonging in each of our souls,
A stage on which we are reminded of hope,
peace, and mercy.

Intimate Knowing
Heard,
Honored,
Seen in a way that transcends our sight,

A classroom in which we are taught patience,
forgiveness, and truth.

Loyal Honesty,
Reality,
Reason,
Words that cultivate the soul within,
A looking-glass in which we are shown trust,
integrity, and identity.

Yourself,
Unyielding,
Unshakable,
Unbreakable vows that steady our footsteps,
A home in which we are upheld in faith, bravery,
and unconditional love.

Moment to Moment

From one moment to the next,
I find myself unsettled and then settled again;
From one heartbeat to the next,
Certainly uncertain in what I don't know;
Each day a flash of possibility,
Of opportunity,
Both seized and allowed to pass by

Yesterday of sorrow,
Of longing,
Of not having a place to belong;
Of wanting a person,
A calling,
A path forward,
Something worthwhile to work on;
Needing the touch of another,
Craving it like air, like food, like breathe;
Feeling empty and alone without it;
Needing action and decision and an immediate
path to follow;
A quick decision and then another,
Never considering the rightness or sense if it,
Just needing to move, move, move

Today of contentment, of peace, of waiting;

Knowing it's coming in timing better than mine,
Trusting in the Giver of Dreams,
Of purpose,
Of faith;
Eagerly waiting,
Contentedly waiting,
Patient and eager to stop and to breath and allow
each moment to crash over me like a wave;
One, another, several, a thousand;
Letting it be and accepting all dreams come with
time

One moment hot, the next minute cold;
Red then blue then something altogether
different;
How patient and kind is the Giver of Dreams to
deal with such an inconstant me;
To give beauty for ashes and purpose for
impatience,
Hopes,
Dreams,
And goals for every flawed moment;
The Consistent in my world of inconsistencies
where tomorrow it will change again;
Once more red then blue then something
altogether different…

Yet always held,
Heard,

Seen,
Called,
Loved;
Always a name to have and a purpose to chase;
Belonging in a home beyond the shores of time
and fragility,
Beyond inconsistencies;
Never alone, never forgotten;
Walking along golden streets with the Giver of
Dreams;
At peace in that eternal moment.

Things I May Never Tell You

You know me, better than most; the genteel
passivity that I emulate and the sharp edges that
I try to pretend don't exist

You've seen the pieces of me that I hold up as
virtue and acceptable and worthy of honor; and
sometimes I can't contain the jagged fragments
of me that I can't seem to control

You know me, better than most; yet here's the
list of what I may never tell you:

I may never tell you that I'm easily angered by
me and that I hate that sometimes my passivity
is born less of a peaceful spirit than it is the
result of wanting to avoid a fight

I may never tell you that I'm torn by feeling so
much at once that it overwhelms me; all at once
my loved ones are my life and yet that sense of
devotion can feel crushing in its intensity

I may never tell you that all I need is a simple
hug because I'm lonely and need someone to
remind me that I'm not truly on my own

I may never tell you that I hate that I can't say
no, especially to those I love the most because I
want to be able to fix the world for you

I may never tell you how much it overwhelms
me when I feel trapped by obligations that I
make because I can't bear to hear someone else
confirm that I once again miscalculated

I may never tell you that I work myself ragged
because I don't know what else I'm supposed to
do to fill the "lack of something" that I feel so
much of each day

And I may never tell you how scared I am of
you ever knowing these things about me because
I'd be heartbroken to watch you choose to walk
away

You know me; better than most and yet there are
things I will never say but hope you hear
somehow and can still chose to stay

There are words I will not speak and thoughts
and fears that I will continue to guard under lock
and key because I'm not yet able to slay that
dragon

Yet, in the list of things I may never tell you,
there is so much more that I will:

I will tell you how much you have changed me
and shaped me and made me better than I was
before; how the person I am now is something I
never could have been on my own

I will tell you that I will always have your back
and that I will help you fight the giants that
come your way because my care for you does
not waver and my loyalty is not easily shattered

I will tell you that there is a deep joy that I
cannot name that has made all the difference in
the storm and burns brighter no matter the
weight of any doubt or trial or thing I may not
tell you

I will tell you that, despite all else, I believe in a
better tomorrow and I believe in the bonds we
build together that get us there; I believe in a
faith, in a love, in a Father that embraces and
lightens even the heaviest of hearts

So while it's true that there are things I may
never tell you, wars that I wage in the silence
and in the unseen corners of my heart and mind,

I have so much more of me that I will choose to
stand in and show to the light

And it remains true that you know me better
than most; the clean and tidy things I like and
the messy, complicated things I don't, I hear the
voice of my Father remind me that perhaps, in
time, with love and trust and growth, there will
come a time when I no longer can say "These
are things I may never tell you"

Music's Man

Have you ever met music's man? Her favorite song? The son who sings the world around him?

If you've never met music's man, allow me to introduce you.

Music's man is the one who sings his world on a scale, of rises and falls that bring many away back into a single tune; not of the rights and wrongs of the average man, but in hills and valleys of melodic beauty.

Rhythms and harmonies are the language he speaks, connecting to each one in a tongue he didn't know he knew; painting murals and mosaics from the voices of many until they sing a single song.

He sees the world around him as a collection of sheets composed by the greatest of the artists; notes and beats called together to create a scene of vivid life; colorful and electric and ceasingly energetic as the music sounds around him!

The one who moves through life this way, this is
music's man; the one to whom the earth dances
and sways to the tune only a few ever hear.

Who can craft symphony from cacophony;
Rhythm from calamity;
Measures, beats, and harmony from the
otherwise seemingly chaotic moments of life.

And what do you get from knowing this man?
Of what should you learn from his life?

To see beauty where it has not yet been
composed;
To see fullness of unity from scattered pieces;
To see potential that the world may miss because
it cannot hear music beckon them.

But music's man can see and hear and respond
to this greatest of music's quests in more ways
than merely one;
To not only see and hear and love his music,
But to give it as a gift to those who know his
name and wish to learn his ways

To impart it, to teach it, to pass it along so that
you too may, one day, be music's man as well.

Pause

Pause, rest, and think;
What makes you thankful?
What causes hesitation;
What stops you in your tracks;
What makes your heart sigh;
To silently thank God for His gifts?

It is the people who fill out the fullness of our
lives;
Who fill in the gaps in between who we are and
who we are becoming;
Who are our laughter, our understanding, our
compassion;
Who make us more of ourselves than we ever
thought we could be.

It is the simple moments that make up our lives;
The meals and time shared;
The jokes made;
The ordinary that, in a crystalline moment,
transform into something extraordinary;
Those golden memories that breathe in us
forever.

It's the humanity in is;

The love of family, friendship, and faith that
become the legacy we leave behind;
The traces of us that remain after we've made
the voyage beyond;
The pictures and stories and laughter that still
live in this form when we no longer do;
It's the image of God in us.

So I ask you again,
What gives you pause?
What stops you in the midst of the everyday, of
the normalcy, of the routine?
What causes your heart to rejoice before you've
even realized you have cause for joy?

It's the faces, the lives, the hearts that live within
our own,
The people who are the vibrant shades of our
time and our love,
The voices that chorus with our own and, rather
than drown us out, magnify us more than we
ever thought possible.

So to the souls who fill in every space of my
life,
Who make me me simply because they are the
joy, the ease, the purpose of my time here,
Who have made me more whole that I ever
dared dream,

Who have taught me who God is through His
love in them…

You are my thanksgiving,
You are my celebration,
You are my heartbeat,
You are my reason and purpose.

Under the Stars

Under the bright shining stars, walked the two
hand in hand,
Silence all around them,
The earth gentle and still

The wind blew past, the last touches of
daylight's heat,
The sweet remnants of sunshine and rain,
The grass soft underfoot

The two looked up, on their walk hand in hand,
The moon shone bright,
Her bright, welcoming face,
The only witness to the two so in love

The fireflies danced to the tune as old as time,
A song sung from creation, yet so seldom heard,
Beautiful music saved and stored,
Made know only to the few who stilled beneath
bright shining stars

She pulled on his hand, her heat glowing bright,
So bright,
The stars swooned in their jealousy

His laugh like the rustling wind, the voice of
spoken promises and vows,
He moved to meet her,
To embrace under pale moonlight's glow

They swayed with the swaying of trees,
A dance with the wind and fields and poppy
blossoms,
A slow step in time with the world's slow turn

They said not a word and they danced,
Turn after turn,
A glow as familiar and warm as the lanterns of
home,
Glowing bright and bidding as the warmth of the
hearth

A slow, distant song as silent and still as the
night,
As steady as a heartbeat, as constant as the stars,
A rhythm and tune as true as the day,
As pure as the night

Turn after turn in the fireflies' glow,
Heartbeat to heartbeat,
Sigh after sigh,
Two as one under a clear, cloudless dome

Their laughs hushed on the breeze,

Time stilled from the tick onward,
Frozen and perfect in flush faced delight,
The sight so lovely and sweet

Their dance beneath the bright shining stars,
Slow and steady, as silent as their heavenly
hosts,
Brilliant, simple, and pure,
Set to the tune of earth's steady hum,
A love song set in motion long before

Enduring, romancing, gently humming,
A song for love and a song for life,
Orchestrated, heard, and danced,
In firefly fields, under the moon's steady gaze,
The two danced and gazed and fell more in love

My Child

There has never been a day when I have not
loved you.

I've held you in my arms, even when you didn't
realize I was there; holding you close to my
heart.

My love brought you into this world; my
precious one, the love of my heart, the
outpouring of my absolute joy.

When you were born, I wept and danced and
shouted for joy that you were; that you breathed
and moved and the air was filled with your first
cries.

I watched you open your eyes for the first time
and see the world anew; I saw every promise
and dream and future reflected in the beautiful
colors of purity and innocence there.

I watched you grow and say your first words; I
watched you tumble and fall as you learned to
walk and laughed with you as you mastered
both; starting to become yourself.

I watched you grow from baby to toddler to
child and teenager; I watched you find every
new facet of yourself and held you as the
growing came in waves of success and failure;
through both the joy and the heartbreak of
living.

I've been here beside you as you have made
your way down this twisting turning path,
through this Labyrinth of being, as you've
become who you are and keep uncovering the
pieces of yourself you haven't found yet.

I have loved you with every ounce of my being
and with every depth of my heart; knowing
always that there is nothing from you that I
would withhold in showing you that my love
comes without limit.

I loved you as I hung on Calvary's tree and laid
aside my very life for you to know that I loved
you; to make it so that you would know I was
there; to know that my love could not be
stopped.

I saw you, my darling child, in every moment
when my cross felt overwhelming and knew that
I would endure all things in order to hold you
close to me; would pay the price demanded so

that you could know how far my love for you
would reach.

I laid down my life for you, and for you I picked
it up again and declared that you were mine. For
you I lived, and have lived, and given you my
name so that you would know whose child you
are.

My love brought you into this world because I
have loved you from beyond the limits of time;
and when you were born I wept and danced and
shouted with joy because you are here and you
live and you are.

I have loved you and watched you grow, even
when you weren't aware that I was there beside
you; holding your hand and walking with you
through the sunshine and thunderstorms of this
life; making new paths for your feet and
growing gardens from ashes.

I have loved you and will continue to love you
even into the very reaches of eternity; laughing
with you as you keep becoming who you are,
holding your hand to help you through the
valleys, and dancing with you on the
mountaintops.

For there has never been a day when I have not loved you.

A Thousand Lifetimes

I've lived a thousand lifetimes in the space of a
single life,
I've journeyed the width and breadth and depth
of the world,
Seen foreign lands, magical worlds,
impossibilities,
All without having ever left my occupied seat

Did you know that the gateway to adventure is
concealed,
Hidden,
Encased,
In the paper white repertoire, the black print of
promise,
Found in between the beginning and the end,
Sitting on the shelf?

Before my time here is through, I will have
known a grand adventure,
The billowing sails of a mighty armada,
Of canon fire and clashing steel,
Of mighty steeds and steadfast heroes,
Of goods and gold that spill through my hands
like water

Of dragon fire and impossible heights,
The intensity of loss and love and that regained,
Of creatures dark and wonderful,
Mythical,
Mystical,
Mystifying,
Of dreams and daydreams and nightmares

I will have known thrill and fear,
Heart racing and stomach tight,
To face down grim death and tell its tale,
To have visited the precipice of insanity,
Of darkness and despair,
And seen the victory of light and love and truth
prevail

Of history, of endless questions,
Of a view of the past that seemingly guides the
future,
Of endless lifetimes endlessly relived,
Of those who came before me, of those who will
come after,
Of those who never were at all

In cathedrals of glass and starlight,
In castles of steel and solid stone,
In fields of unending light and waves,
In the dwelling places where reside both chaos
and creation

Before my own departure I will have lived and
died a hundred fold,
A thousand lifetimes, come and gone,
Clothed in mere parchment and ink,
Draped in the riches of kings,
The rags of paupers,
Known in a million worlds by a million names

And then in an instant I am returned to myself,
My seat still occupied,
Unmoved,
Days and weeks traded for simple hours held in
my hands,
And altogether I remain unchanged while yet
entirely altered,
The sight before me returned as if the one seen
had never existed at all

And to it I return time and time again,
Eager,
Breathless,
Exhilarated at the next destination before me,
Simple and vast, a universe amongst the
collection held in my hands,
And I set to it again, footstep by footstep,
Line by line
Off to live my next lifetime within my own
walls

Color Blind

I used to think the world needed more color in it;
Less of the gray spaces, less of the monotone;
Yet, I don't wish for color anymore;
I wish for colorblindness

I wish for a world where black and white are
only hues of shading;
Equals and companions that they were in my
childhood art class;
Beautiful, bold sketches that created a whole
image;
Now they are battle lines, drawn in a fight to be
heard;
They are the cause of riots, hatred, oppression;
They tell me that one life should be valued over
another, fought for over another;
Defended, supported, and respected over
another;
Where they are not together equal works of the
same art…

I wish for a world where red and blue are only
hues of vibrancy;
Tools meant to bring the picture off of the page;

To reflect the brushstrokes of a sunrise sky and a
calm ocean depth;
Now they are platforms by which one person
condemns another;
They are divisions between families and friends,
coworkers, and society;
They tell me that no matter what ideas I hold in
my head, I value wrong and I think wrong and I
am aligned wrong;
That one fights to wash the world completely of
the other until it is the only one left;
Where they are not together both striking and
beautiful in their balance…

I wish for a world where color palates are only
hues of the brush;
Combinations of the easel's ability to facilitate
an artist's work;
To bring visions to life that make the picture
whole;
Now they are banners flown to defend the camp
of who I do or do not take to my bed;
They are the army of which war we are enlisting
to fight in, to be defined by, to lay down
everything for;
They tell me that I must fight and speak and die
for one so that my enemy will know who I am
inside;
They are our chosen names;

Where they are not together the colors of a
whole artwork filled out to be whole…

I used to wish the world had more colors in it;
That is until I learned that colors are only skin
tone, politics, and gender in this world;
A once beautiful, diverse, colorful painting
divided by everything that colors were never
meant to be;
Given meaning they were never meant to have;
Used in the destruction of art rather than the
creation of it;
No longer enthralling dark mountain peaks
caped with dazzling snow;
No longer beautiful fields of flowers draped
against a stunning sky;
No longer the symbols of hope for all of
humanity;
Only division, only hatred;
Only a world of sides to be taken and wars to
win…

I no longer wish for more colors, but fewer;
I no longer wish for more distinct hues, but more
overlap until one is indistinguishable from
another;
I no longer wish to see each individual vibrancy,
but the image as a whole;

I now wish for colorblindness in the hopes that, in it, the world may once again be filled with colors of beauty…

Autumn

It's time again, the wind turned chill and the
seasons change.
Warmth, sun, endless ease,
Replaced by old, crisp leaves upon the ground,
A new sense in the air,
A change in the mood.

The smells of sunscreen and BBQs and hazy
heat replaced again by familiar, long awaited
friends.
The scents of spice and pumpkin and apple
come in strong on the breeze,
Of hay and cloth and newly harvested earth.

The colors change; the world born into a new
hue.
The neons and brights traded in for darker
shades and warmer feels,
Even the trees and fields turning in their summer
coats for autumn's lens.

People feel it in the air, the change as decadent
and rich,
Soothing and bracing and bold,
As the coffee and drink so strong,

So welcoming,
That marks the change in year.

Quickly lawn chairs and swimsuits are returned
to closet depths,
Saved and forgotten,
Replaced by lamb's wool and knitted embrace,
The world swaddled and swathed for the new.

Soon candy and costume,
Pumpkins and gourdes,
Will line the streets and adorn the homes of each
and every neighbor,
Sentinels of autumn time joys,
Keepers of the newly budding season.

Characters and new forms appear,
As common, as welcomed, as birds in the air,
Merriment and amusement,
Parties and pairings of costumed connections,
Delighting in the ring of each doorbell and
shouted exclamation

Then, football and the roasting of turkey,
Ciders and spreads,
Food and family and gatherings galore,
Autumnal glee and graciousness,
Turning strangers into friends

Meals that bind us one to another,
With feelings of graciousness and thanks
abounding,
Long awaited arrivals of those far from home,
An appreciated pause from business and work,
A time for rest, reflection, and cheery

On the doorstep to merriment of an altogether
different kind as winter prepares for its yearly
debut

But for now, autumn is king,
Embraced and delighted,
Slow and steady,
Cool and calm,
A gentle hum of anticipation,
A time to stop, to still, to enjoy
Autumn is here for its moment again

Life by the Clock

Eyes on the clock,
Tick-tock, tick-tock,
Hours creep by,
Hours fly by,
Tick-tock, tick-tock

We are people who live by the clock,
Each morning the alarm goes off,
Beep, beep, beep,
Time to start another day,
When to get up?
When to leave the house?
Do I have time for food?
Did I pack a lunch?
Do I have everything with me?
Beep, beep, beep

Traffic starts are the engine roars,
Car to car,
Bumper to bumper,
Honk, honk, honk,
The clock continues to tick-tock forward,
Will I be late?
Why aren't we moving?
Why can noone drive?

Can I get to work,
To school,
To anywhere on time?
Honk, honk, honk

Biund to the desk,
My world for the day,
The pen on paper,
The keyboard's click,
Clack, clack, clack,
Information coming,
Information going,
My thoughts humming as I scribble away,
My heartbeat matching the sound of time
passing,
Is this project done right?
Why are we in this meeting?
Is time moving slower?
Why isn't it lunch yet?
Clack, clack, clack

Finally, finally the work day is done,
Pick-ups and drop-offs keep us running,
School done, now sports, arts, activities,
Work done, now chores,
The clock continues to eat away at leisure time,
Vroom, vroom, vroom
Did we eat dinner?
How late is your practice?

Do we have time to go home first?
Can we just grab food?
Did you remember your uniform, your script,
your things?
If I go here, can you go there?
Vroom, vroom, vroom

Quick setting sun,
Finally home,
Have to wash, have to plan, have to pack,
All to satisfy tomorrow's clock,
Scrub, Scrub, Scrub
Clothes to be cleaned,
Homework to be done,
Lunches to be packed,
Have you showered?
Is your homework done?
Did you brush your teeth?
Are you ready for work tomorrow?
Scrub, scrub, scrub

Laying down at last,
Heartbeat thundering,
Mind still racing,
Eyes staring into the darkness,
Blink, Blink, Blink
Time still ticking by,
Why can't I sleep?
Why can't I still?

Why is my head so loud?
Did I do this?
Did I do that?
How many hours left until the alarm?
Blink, Blink, blink

Eyes on the clock,
Tick-tock, tick-tock,
Hours creep by,
Hours fly by,
Tick-tock, tick tock

For You

For you, my love, what can I give? What token
can I leave you with to know how much my
heart has beat for you when words are not
enough? What do I give as my embrace when
my embrace is far away?

Gifts of gold and silver, of wealth and material
things; gifts that exist in the night, yet evaporate
as quickly as the dew is gone with the rising
sun?
No, such things could never do!

Instead, Here is the gift I give to you:

I give you the space of my mind; to keep your
face always close to me in my waking as much
as in my sleeping, to give you each
consideration and mindfulness of my thought,
and to always hold your benefit above my own
in each idea and dream for the future.

I give you the wholeness of myself; to value you
in every characteristic of who you are, to support
and aid you within every inch of my own

character, and to guard you with each and every ability given to me that makes me me.

I give you the work of my hands; to build a home of dependability and security and safety, to provide alongside you for each and every need, and to meet each day with the willingness to fight what battles we may face.

And even above each of these things, I give you the very love of my heart; to love and adore and accept you through each and every moment, to listen and feel and share each triumph and trial, and to give you that which is the very pulse in my veins.

Each of these I give you, for these are the gifts of love. Not of infatuation or desire or rose-tinted positivity, but of that which binds one heart to another for a lifetime.

I give you that which is mine to give, and that which nothing on earth can tarnish or steal or shatter. This is my gift, my promise, my vow. To you. With you. For you.

Firefly Hill

There's a spot that I know,
Where lights come to dance,
Where fireflies gather,
Where they cause quite a trance

It's a small little hill,
On the outside of town,
Many walk straight on by it,
Marked with a frown

They don't understand
This magical place,
That appears after sundown,
Where they gather, they race

The fireflies come,
They come in their droves,
They come to light darkness,
They glow in their groves

They dance to a tune
So rarely to hear,
They dance in the starlight
They dance for you, dear

For lovers they glow,
To those out after dark,
They glow for sweet couples,
Out now in the park

They glow for the small ones,
Whose eyes are so sweet,
They glow for small children,
Their laughter a treat

They glow for the innocents,
They glow for the old,
They glow for all people
Who come weak and come bold

If you know where to find them
They'll dance for you too,
They'll dance for your gladness
If you're mad, if you're blue

A light in the dark,
A signpost of hope,
The fireflies glitter
They draw in like rope

They dwell on their hill
Simply waiting for night
They glow in the darkness
To drive away fright

It's a sight great to see
It bolsters the soul
They dance oh so gently
They swoop as you stroll

This magical place
Will give you a thrill
A sight sure to soothe you,
This firefly hill

Snow

Relentless,
Fierce,
Frozen,
Impassive,
Decisive as it howls and freezes, claiming its
time.

Silent,
Still,
Quiet,
Peaceful,
Gentle as it dusts the face of tree and street and
home.

Relentless,
Fierce,
Frozen,
Impassive as it rages on with disregard for safety
or comfort or ease,
Decisive.

Silent,
Still,
Quiet,

Peaceful as the world pauses, stops, to take a
collective breath,
Gentle.

Relentless,
Fierce,
Frozen as the ground gives up its fields of
flowers for fields of unceasing white,
Impassive,
Decisive.

Silent,
Still,
Quiet as the wind swiftly, stealthily, dances
through branches and archways and open air,
Peaceful,
Gentle.

Relentless,
Fierce as the sound of cracking ice and howling
wind that chill soul as well as earth,
Frozen,
Impassive,
Decisive.

Silent,
Still as the inside of a steeple, hushed and bowed
in reverent reflection,
Quiet,

Peaceful,
Gentle.

Relentless as sound enfolds into its grasp and
color dissolves before it,
Fierce,
Frozen,
Impassive,
Decisive.

Silent as midnight, the earth asleep under its
familiar, charming, embracing blanket,
Still,
Quiet,
Peaceful,
Gentle.

Day at the Beach

Day at the beach,
How I dream of such joy
Day at the beach,
Better than some electronic toy

I long for the water,
It's continuous crash,
The funfair of the boardwalk,
A great place to spend cash

The hot, sunbaked shore
Where sandcastles grow,
Pale and shovels abound,
Happy faces aglow

We surf and we swim,
We play games in the sand,
We run, shout, and laugh,
We have a time that is grand

Seashells are scattered,
There here and about,
We collect all we can find,
We will find them, no doubt

As the sun starts to set,
As the day turns to dusk,
We begin our bonfire revelry,
As the wind comes up brusque

There is food and sweet treats,
We may sing some songs,
We gather close together,
Knowing each one belongs

How I dream of sweet visions
Spent freely and fun,
How I long for a beach day,
To bask in summer's warm sun

But it's wintertime now,
I'm far from such days,
I have to bundle up warmly,
Inside everyone stays

But I'm dreaming of beach trips,
To get me to through snow
I'm dreaming of beach days,
While winter winds blow

And when summer returns,
When it's finally hot
I'll have my great beach day
With winter forgot

Marvelously Made

I am a human being, fearfully and wonderfully made in the image of my Father, crafted by the hand of the Creator.
I am a Christian, a soldier, a foreigner in this land, proudly and humbly bearing my Redeemer's name.
I am a daughter, my mom and dad's child lovingly raised and nurtured to value this life.
I am a sister, the younger of two, bonded with another who bears and understands the scars that we share.
I am a friend, a kindred spirit with others who may not share my blood or my name, yet are the tribe of my heart.
I am an aunt, entrusted with the shared care and direction of another's child, being sister and mentor and friend all at once.
I am a leader, made and impassioned to serve the ones that Jesus called to Himself and bade the disciples to never hinder.
I am a theologian, someone who sacredly values the pursuit of God's Word, the Scriptures, and a genuine relationship with The Rock of All Ages.

I am a teacher, enabled to share that which I
know so that others may be wiser than me, and
to do better than I have done.

I am all of these things, and so many more, that
my God has made me to be; these things that He
has instilled in my being and my soul. They are
my Holy Spirit calling, the work He prepared for
me to do long before I'd drawn my first breath
on my first day. They are the sacred and
undeniable name that He has given me, and I
will not spend even another day pretending as if
they are not.
To Him my life is given up, and in His ways I
shall walk, even imperfectly, even failingly so. If
this be the person He has made, lovingly and
sure handedly, who am I to claim mistake? Do I
claim there to be fault in He who is without
fault? No, not for another day.

Lovingly.
Purposefully.
Fearfully.
Wonderfully.
Intentionally.

To praise.
To worship.
To pray.

To pursue.
To belong to.

"I thank you, High God-you're breathtaking!
Body and soul, I am marvelously made!"

Scotland

O land of mist ensconced delight,
Of wild glens and soaring peaks,
Crystal waters to chill the bone,
And amber fire to warm the soul

Faerie stories to mystify each man,
Their mysteries and magic unfold,
Set to enrapture the country's mind,
As the enduring legacies of old,
Old as the rock and stone upon,
Where legends are birthed,
Upon which heroes endure,
From one memory to the next

Clear blue lochs under azure skies,
Emerald fields dotted in lavender heather,
Castles and keeps built upon family ties,
Lost and found so to be lost again,
The blood of Lairds and Ladies,
The heartbeat of history

The poet's cradle and healing's home,
Royal miles the first and last,
Keeping to the pulse of palaces,
A vanguard of pride and passion,

Of prince's fancy and king's resolve,
To endure,
To rise,
To fight,
To never die

O land of mist ensconced delight,
Of wild glens and soaring peaks,
Crystal waters to chill the bone,
And amber fire to warm the soul

In days gone by,
In feasts of fires,
Of renewal, of re birth, of time unto time,
The Celtic call to worlds unseen,
Food and bemusement, chants and beckonings,
Music on the wind,
Startling and serene,
As sung by the voices of the past

The lowing and bleeting of kine and jumbuck,
The fields filled with the soul of a loving life,
Draped in warmth to warm the many,
Sounding out the sounds of home and hearth,
Of generations back and everlasting ritual

The piper's tune pervades the breeze,
Warm and brash,
Pure and strong,

The constant cadence of valor's onward march,
Proud and bold as thistle's sting,
A valiant steed of highland renown,
Defiant and true in the graze of lion's claw

O land of mist ensconced delight,
Of wild glens and soaring peaks,
Crystal waters to chill the bone,
And amber fire to warm the soul

Scotland is her name

Peace

Heartbeat pounding, thump, thump, thump,
Like an unstoppable jackhammer thundering in
my chest

An unquiet mind, a mean, nasty, cruel mind,
A voice spewing every fear, every darkest held
insecurity bubbling up in my head

There is no ease in sleep; wicked, taunting
dreams dance across my eyelids and I wake
from fitful rest drenched in sweat,
Thump, thump, thump

My clothes fit just too tight around my neck,
My limbs ache and yearn to run, run, run
Go where they can't find us, can't hurt us

Screaming in the stillness, too quiet, too quiet
Faces, images, every though visible in the
darkness, the night no place to hide, only to
suffer, to wait until daylight

My most beloved things now my greatest fears;
my voices of reason screaming for blood, for

recompense, for my heart removed from my
chest.

Air is too thick, too warm, too cold,
Every sensation excruciating on my skin,
The softest and safest now the cruelest and most
suffocating

Will it end? Who can make it end? Darkness too
dark, brightness too bright, no relief,
No silence or comfort, just thump, thump, thump
Chipping away the bone in my chest

Queasy, overwhelmed, overtaken, drowning in a
sea of whispers I can't make stop; monsters in
the place of familiarity, a hollow stomach on the
edge of sickness

No distraction strong enough, no image a harbor
in the raging storm of heart and mind and still
chaos; no mute button, no pause, no volume
down,
Only louder, louder, louder with each passing
tick, tick, tick of the clock

Will it stop? Please, let it stop…

And then, a stillness, a comfort, a peace;
unstoppable, illogical, unexplainable.

A still quiet voice louder than the thundering
chorus inside.
The spark of stillness amidst the rolling waves.

Be at ease.
Be stilled.
Peace.
Peace.

As suddenly as the tidal waves crashed, they
recede; a voice commanding them back to the
bounds of their place.

Softness to replace that which was harsh.
Gentleness to replace the cruelty.
A commanding voice to silence it all, even the
deafening thump, thump, thump.

Be at ease.
Be stilled.
Peace.
Peace.

You are whole. You are safe. You are more than
the sum of the fears. Light for your darkness.
Beauty for ashes.

Seen.
Loved.

Held.
Healed.

Suddenly the night is quiet once more. The
shadows suddenly tamed beneath the Master's
call.
The air cool and the blanket warm, an embrace,
a comfort for a calming heart; a gentle touch.
Dreams anew with loving care.

Sleep now.
Sleep.
Be at ease.
Be stilled.
Peace.
Peace.

Beautiful Morning

The dawn broke so early,
The air impossibly still,
The world waiting, waiting, waiting,
For the next act in the Writer's great play

It was still on the grounds,
Only the tombs standing watch,
Not a breath could be heard,
No birdsong to usher in hope

They came slowly and somberly,
Arms laden with herbs,
To what had yet to be done,
That which had been hastily seen to

The darkness had been suffocating,
Unbelievable, frightening, unreal,
A sight no one has ever imagined they'd see,
Their teacher, their friend, a lamb given

His voice still rang in their ears,
In their hearts,
As they made the slow march to death's grim
doorstep,
The doormat where light lay slain

Yet, the sight was surprising when their path was
finished,
An anomaly before their eyes,
Unexplainable, Inexplicable,
Who could come to account?

The sacred resting place disturbed,
The stone rolled away,
Only linen wrappings left,
An empty grave in the midst of the garden

Worry and heartbreak,
Now newly fresh,
Filled up their hearts and their heads,
Who of even the worst could stood as low as the
sight before them?

Yet this was the dawning of eternal bound life,
Something to change them all completely,
Each who had ever met this unworldly Man,
Who bore the titles of hope of generations past

Then they saw the strangest of sights,
So casually lounging on death's slab of bed,
This man dressed in white,
Light his companion and witness to this new era
come

Why do you search for living amongst death,

Do you not remember the Word's words,
His promise,
His pronouncement of I AM's plans?

The One you seek is not here,
For this is victory's day,
Over the slavers of sin and shame and darkness,
Overthrown by Love's love and Passover care!

And as these strange words stirred the hearts of
its hearers,
The world shifted upward,
Full of bright promise and giftings of love's
perfect form,
Looking up they were joined by He who they
grieved

Hope was alive, well, and whole,
Death's day had been thwarted,
Condemned to its own punishment,
Bowed low before heaven's Master

Why do you weep? Why do you cry?
I am here with you,
Victorious, living, successful in mission,
I've died every death and bought life for you
unending

I've made you wholly new from time unto time,

In me you are washed and cleansed, clean, and
unblemished,
Because of my life, my death, and my life once
more reclaimed,
You belong here no longer and have new hope to
endure

And from that beautiful garden, that beautiful
morning,
News spread on the four winds,
Fast and furious as thundering feet could go,
From land unto land and sea unto sea

Have you heard the Good News that death has
died?
Have you heard that salvation is living among
men?
That one simple gift, and act of unmatched love,
Has bought you free from that which owned
you?

He is the Light of the World,
Love's perfect perfector,
The Passover Lamb,
The Commander of Heaven's Armies

He has bought you sweet freedom,
Paid dearly on a rugged, worn cross,
Conquered world's ruthless revolt,

To open heaven's bright shining gates

It was a beautiful morning when the world
completely changed,
When death bowed to life in its war lost,
When the God of all time declared freedom for
all,
With the gift of His life, unbroken, reclaimed,
eternal

He calls you, He calls me,
He offers His life,
As the price for my heartlessness,
To be born again now

To bear witness to the beautiful morning,
To sing its song on the wings of the winds,
To teaching it to the world's waiting souls
To keep it enduring to endless generations

An Ode to a Strong Woman

Who is she, this woman,
A pillar of strength, an emblem of grace,
She rides into battle,
Undaunted,
Unyielding,
A warrior, a storm

She's a mother, a daughter,
A sister, a friend,
She is your confidant, your mentor,
Wise,
Mischievous,
A shoulder to cry on and shelter for comfort

She's the forger of paths and doer of justice,
She's fierce and she's kind,
She's a force to contend with,
Uncontainable,
Beautiful,
Your champion when there's a fight to be fought

She can do all the things you think she cannot,
She is unstoppable in her nature,
She's as driven and determined as the wind,
Fierce,

Confident,
She's the pillar for many she may never realize

But she's gentle and soft under her armor,
She's loving and so peacefully kind,
A voice of compassion and grace,
Understanding,
Discerning,
A place of relief for other warriors' rest

Remember to care for her,
To relieve her of her burden every now and
again,
To let her be carried rather than carrying,
Restful,
Relaxed,
Care for her soldiering heart, for her
burdenedsome back

The woman of strength is a fiercely fought foe,
Should you find yourself in her crosshairs,
In the focus of her sights,
Determined,
Unstoppable,
You better find shelter from the undimmable
storm

You know her, you've seen her,
She's born from a hard treaded path,

From the grips of hardship and unchangeable
grit,
Powerful,
Victorious,
A woman who makes women strong like herself

To all of the strong women in this unfriendly
world,
To the leaders and defenders,
To all who have had their voice challenged,
Speak loud,
Speak out,
Stay the strong women our world deeply needs

Calloused Hands & A Tender Heart

One life; a finite set of years; a single
opportunity to let them know that I was here;
how do I let them know I was here?

Should I strive for a legacy of financial success
and material wealth? To invent and to create and
to build up an empire that ends in multiple
zeros? Leave behind a bank account to leave
even the 1% speechless?

Should I seek out my chance for fame and
notoriety? Be a face, a figure, an elite for the
sake of making art or music or film? Be a
household name among those whose names I'll
never know?

No, no; that isn't my gift to leave behind, that
isn't the purpose of my time. I seek something
that will never rust or break or fade; a legacy
built on a solid foundation to last a thousand
generations.

I seek to leave behind the thoughts of my mind
so that they may sow much more than intellect;

but that they would sow a thoughtfulness,
consideration, and creativity that turns a
destructive detachment to a constructive
awareness.

I seek to leave behind the passions of my soul so
that they would sow much more than ambition;
but that they would sow a justice, safety, and
compassion that transforms a narrow-minded
reaction into a life-giving action.

I seek to leave behind the work of my hands that
they may sow much more than accomplishment;
but that they would sow a gentleness, empathy,
and generosity that trades in a self-benefitting
complacency for a selfless responsibility.

I seek to leave behind the seasons of my heart
that they may sow much more than fleeting
emotions; but that they would sow a mercy,
forgiveness, and grace that breaks the walls of
hardened skepticism and exposes a softened
spirit of hope.

One life; a finite set of years; a single
opportunity to let them know that I was here; let
these be the ways I let them know was here; a
legacy of spirit defined by love and goodness.

At my end, in the light of the setting sun of my
life, my time, my finite set of years, let me be
remembered by calloused hands and a tender
heart.